NEW YORK

BONECHI

*Everyone wants to make it in New York and everyone's trying to. That's the main source of the enormous energy of New York City. **The Big Apple**, jazz musicians call it. All sorts of people from all over the world speaking every known language, jostling each other in the streets and the subway, traying to make it. The moment you find somewhere to live, no matter how grotty, or how expensive, the moment you go to work, you begin to be a New Yorker. The more work you do and the less prejudice you have about other tongues and other people and other ways, the more a New Yorker you become.*

Sole Agents in North America:
IPS - International Promotion Service, Inc.
634 Rosalia Street
ATLANTA, GA 30312
Tel. (404) 622-1692 - Fax. (404) 622-1692

Text by: RICHARD FREMANTLE

Photographs from the Archives of Casa Editrice Bonechi taken by

PAOLO GIAMBONE: pages 24 b,c, 31, 37, 38, 39, 40, 42, 43, 46 b, 47 b, 48, 49, 52 c, 54.

ANDREA PISTOLESI: pages 3, 4, 5, 6, 7, 8-9, 10,11,12, 13, 14, 15, 16, 17, 18, 19, 20, 21, 22, 23, 24 a, 25, 26, 27, 28, 29, 30, 32, 33, 34, 35, 36, 41, 44, 45, 46 a, c, 47 a, c, 50, 51, 52 a, b, 53, 55, 56, 57, 58, 59, 60, 61, 62, 63.

ISBN 88-8029-128-9

Lower Manhattan seen from *Upper Bay*.

NEW YORK

New York is the world's capital, not because its financial district is the most important, or its shops the best, or its publishers the biggest, or its port the finest, but because New York is made up of everyone: **Mr Everyman** from all over the planet. And maybe even a few beings from other planets... New York's character has always come from the vast immigrations which even today are being absorbed into the city.

To be a New Yorker you don't – as you do in Paris, or London, or Tokyo – have to speak in a certain way or dress in a certain way or be educated in this or that. In New York you can be anyone from anywhere, and still be a New Yorker. In that way, in its lack of effective prejudice, it's the least middle-class town in the world.

This lack of unifying culture leads many visitors, usually the wealthier ones, to see New York as a cold town, maybe even a place they don't like. But it's exactly that freedom from obligatory forms which has always made New York so open, dynamic, and even warm – not so much for the haves, but for the have-nots. Or anyway for all those people from all walks of life who prefer not to hide behind the prejudices or the so-called privileges of their own particular background.

If you think your ways or your language or culture are better, New York's not for you. If you have an open mind to any form that any idea might take, New York's the most exciting city in the world. It's that simple – take New York as it is, release your own prejudices, and you enter into the spirit which makes the town unique.

New York City at night. *In the center is the **Empire State Building**, and just to its right are the two **World Trade** towers. To the right of them is the Upper Bay.*

*When. the **Chrysler Building** was finished in 1930, it was the tallest skyscraper in the world, and is still now one of the most famous.*

The Upper East Side, Grove Street in the Village, Chinatown, Lincoln Center, Columbia University – each part of New York is a neighborhood unto itself which has nothing to join it to all the others except its people; no particular tongue, no accent, no manner of behaving or dressing. New York is made up of neighborhoods and each neighborhood is made of the layers of its past immigrations. Each is calm, residential and individual, living quietly under the overlying common web of energy which drives the city forward each day. Most visitors miss this neighborly quality of New York and see only the energy.

Manhattan Island. To most people New York means Manhattan. And until 1898, when the other four boroughs – Brooklyn, the Bronx, Queens and Richmond (or Staten Island) – were joined to it, this was true. That's why the Manhattan postal address is still **New York, New York**.

New York is, and always has been, an immigrant town, and a port. The early settlers – Dutch, English, Scots and Germans – were followed in the nineteenth century by enormous waves of Germans and Irish. Then in our own century Italians, Jews from all over Europe – but particularly from Russia, Poland, the Baltic States

and Germany, – Black Americans from the South of the United States, Puerto Ricans, and Hungarians have followed each other by the millions to the city. Most recently the immigrations have come from all the countries of the Caribbean and Latin America, and from South-East Asia – particularly Viet-nam. Almost every successive immigration has been forced onto the bottom rung of the social ladder, until a new one pushed it upwards, often instilling an unfortunate superior, racist attitude towards the newer arrivals, with an accompanying tension.

*On this and facing page: two views of the **Empire State Building** and a detail of the decoration inside.*

Following pages:

*Panoramic view of lower **Midtown Manhattan**. The **East River** is in the foreground, with the 34th St. heliport, and the **East River Drive**. Straight ahead is the **Empire State Building**, and to the right are some of the skyscrapers and large apartment blocks in lower Midtown. Beyond the Empire State Building is the Hudson River and beyond that, New Jersey.*

New York is primarily a city on water. Of the five boroughs, Manhattan and Staten Island are islands, Brooklyn and Queens are on the western most end of the large island called Long Island, and the Bronx is a peninsula surrounded on three sides by water. The city's bays and rivers not only form one of the world's greatest and most beautiful natural harbours, but they've always provided much of the city's tremendous energy and its extraordinary growth.

To the north the freshwater Hudson River, a mile wide at Manhattan, leads far inland to upstate New York and to the Erie Canal. The Canal in turn leads to the Great Lakes so that – since 1825 when it opened – people and goods can travel easily to Detroit, Chicago, Milwaukee and Canada. This reach into the heart of the whole North American Continent is an essential part of New York's cosmopolitan feeling.

To the East, along the East River and through Long Island Sound, the whole New England coast of Connecticut, Rhode Island and Massachusetts are accessible, mostly through protected waters.

From 1892 to 1924 **Ellis Island** which is now a national
monument, was where immigrants were first received. The
Ellis Island Immigration Museum, inaugurated in 1930, is
housed in the main building, which was recently restored.

Facing page and on the following pages:

The Statue of Liberty, symbol of all the millions of immigrants
who have found a new home in America. The Upper Bay is
behind, New Jersey beyond. Dedicated in 1885, the Statue was
designed by the French sculptor, Auguste Bartholdi, and shipped
in pieces from Paris to New York. From windows in the crown
the views over the Bay are magnificent.

Although the surface area of the water within the
city is less than that of the land, the sizeable
lake-like area of the Hudson and the Upper Bay
have also been essential to New York's growth
and prosperity. New York's beautiful bays and
rivers are the unheralded source of the city's
uniqueness – not only its lung, but reflecting its
grand, unfettered mind.

To the South, the Atlantic has always made
transport easy along the American continent to
the Gulf of Mexico, as well as to Europe and
Africa. New Yorkers are unconsciously always
aware that they live and work on the edge of the
formidable expanse of the Atlantic Ocean, its vast
energy: their own private lake, they might
observe...

Views of Rockefeller Center, built in the 1930's, and its Statue of Prometheus. In the summer part of the plaza is a café; in the winter an ice-skating rink. The promenade towards 5th Avenue is decorated with flowers and water.

How to see the city. An ideal way to see New York today is from the right or starboard side of flights into La Guardia airport originating in the South and West of the country. If lucky, these flights bank over the Statue of Liberty as though saluting that world symbol of freedom, to fly right up the Hudson before turning east over the north of Manhattan. The whole of Manhattan, Brooklyn and Queens float majestically below. The Lower Bay with Governor's Island and the East River's bridges being successively succeeded by the great towers on the tip of Manhattan, then by the lower residential buildings of the streets numbered in the twentys and thirtys, and the enormous number of skyscrapers in Midtown. Like a planned secret garden, the vast green area of Central Park follows, with its lake and the cliff-like quality of the buildings on its edge. The park is succeeded by Columbia University on Morningside Heights, the tenements of Harlem to the University's east, the Harlem River and the opening into Long Island Sound beyond.

In the old days, until the late sixties, the main route into New York was as striking as the plane's view but slower and more stately. Ships great and small sailed and steamed across the Lower Bay through the Verrazano Narrows into the breathtakingly beautiful harbour of the Upper Bay: Staten Island to the port, Lower Manhattan and the Hudson River directly ahead, Brooklyn and Queens to the starboard.

Even today New York is primarily a port – a port of people as well as goods. Some forty to fifty per cent of the city's population is still foreign-born or born of foreign-born parents. New York's a trading city, a business city, a gateway into the United States for energy, and the products of energy, from all over the world. New York can be called the world's capital because paradoxically this city is not actually the capital of anywhere, not even the State of New York which has its capital at Albany, some one hundred and fifty miles up the Hudson. Symbolically, New York is the site of the **United Nations**, the only world government – no matter how often timid and ineffectual – we have.

*A detail of **Rockefeller Center**.*

Following pages:
*two pictures of the **Statue of Prometheus** which dominates the **Lower Plaza** in Rockefeller Center, one taken in summer, the other in winter.*

*The fountain outside the **Exxon Building** on 6th Avenue, opposite **Radio City Music Hall**.*

*Radio City Music Hall** and the **RCA Building** at Rockefeller Center.*

Although not a capital, New York is far and away the most important city in the United States – economically, culturally and socially. And it's obviously also the most important city in New York State – which by itself has a population and an economy greater than many of the world's nations. Until New York State was overtaken by California in the 1960's it was by all measures the number one state in the Union, – an enormous area of almost 50,000 square miles (over half the size of Great Britain, for instance), which boasts lovely unspoiled hills and mountains in the Catskills and Adirondacks, nine major rivers and some 8,000 lakes. And which has 127 miles of Atlantic coast and 371 miles of shore line on Lakes Erie and Ontario, as well as the American side of Niagara Falls.

Even though the Port of New York Authority sees far fewer ships than in the past, New York's three large and many smaller airports make up, in the movement of people and goods, for what has been lost in water commerce. The port, by itself over 1200 kilometers of waterfront with a capacity for almost four hundred ships, together with La Guardia, JFK and Newark airports, still make New York the greatest single port in the world.

New York is a city of work. The garment industry, the media, and government are the biggest employers. Contrary to what many visitors feel, New York spends more on social services than any other major city in the United States. The reason that the opposite often appears to be the case is that New York has not only some of the richest people in the world, it also has vast armies of the poorest.

And, although visitors often feel that New York is violent, few New Yorkers would agree. At one end of a small island only about eleven miles long is Wall Street with all its enormous capitalistic wealth, its yuppies, and, often, its manipulators and greed. At the other end is Harlem with its burned-out buildings, its unused talents, its rich soul and abject poverty. In between are literally millions of poor, energetic, needful immigrants, often not speaking English or

EXPERIENCE THE DIVINE
BETTE MIDLER
RADIO CITY
MUSIC HALL
RADIO CITY
NCE THE DIVINE BETTE MIDLER NOW THRU 10/23

St Patrick's Cathedral on 5th Avenue between 50th and 51st Streets. Built in the neo-Gothic style in the 1880's this is the major Roman Catholic Church of New York. It stands opposite Rockefeller Center, and is here seen through the Statue of Atlas – Material and Spiritual Christian power.

A detail of the neo-Gothic interior of **St. Patrick's Cathedral**.

The **International Building of Rockefeller Center**, photographed through the **Statue of Atlas**, is located behind 5th Avenue, between 50th and 51st Street.

even Spanish, often desperate. And all around Manhattan and on it, lives the biggest port and single tourist center in the world, as well as the centers of many national and international crime and drug rings, local gangs and vice purveyors on a massive scale... There's a good argument that, considering its circumstances, New York is a remarkably non-violent city, where the hard-working people, the neighborliness, the striking beauty, both by day and at night, the pleasure of fine living, the intelligence and wonderful education of many New Yorkers – are all infinitely more important than the very moderate level of violence.

Three pictures of skyscrapers, seen from various points of view.

New York is a city of communications: the **New York Times** is one of the major newspapers of the world, and many major magazines such as **Time** and **Vogue** and **The New Yorker** have their headquarters in New York. The city is also home to much that is best or biggest in publishing, as well as to many major radio, TV and film companies. A list of the names of some of the new skyscrapers in Midtown alone gives an idea of the diverse corporate power which works every day in New York City: Gulf & Western, J.C. Penney, Exxon, McGraw-Hill, Celanese, N.Y. Telephone, RCA, CBS, ABC, Squibb, Sperry-Rand, Associated Press, Warners, IBM, A T & T, Segram, Lever, General Motors, Harper & Row, Citicorp, General Electric, Chemical Bank, PanAmerican, National Distillers, Macmillan.

Yet New York is governed by the common man.
No elite bureaucratic class of any kind exists.
The mayor and major officials of the world's most
powerful city have traditionally come from every
sort of background. The names of some of the last
mayors, La Guardia, O'Dwyer, Lindsay and Koch,
give an idea of the many ethnic backgrounds of
the city's officials. New York government, like
America as a whole, is one of the greatest, most
exciting experiments in democracy ever
attempted by man.

Shopping in New York. Because of the
ramifications of its vast trade, particularly the
garment and beauty industries, New York is a
city to shop in. Some of the most famous stores in
the world are found in Manhattan – Tiffany's,

*Below, **City Hall**, built between 1802 and 1811 in line with
the neo-classic taste of the times. The **statue
of Lady Justice** rising up over the metal dome.*

Typical New York street scenes. *Hot-dog and orangeade venders, a West Indian making music and the famous yellow cabs of New York.*

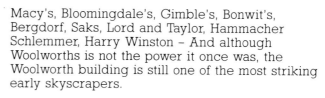

Macy's, Bloomingdale's, Gimble's, Bonwit's, Bergdorf, Saks, Lord and Taylor, Hammacher Schlemmer, Harry Winston – And although Woolworths is not the power it once was, the Woolworth building is still one of the most striking early skyscrapers.

Nowadays a lot of the best shops are foreign. Madison Avenue in particular is lined with dozens of chic Italian fashion houses, a fine counterpoise to the **Little Italy** remnant in the city of another less prosperous period in Italian history. Good bookshops also abound, particularly used book ones where many hours may be passed browsing, with no obligation to buy.

New York architecture is the ultimate reflection of the power of business in New York and an illustration of how art grows out of trade. No known building effort in the whole history of man,

__Two views of the United Nations Headquarters__ on the East River between 42nd and 47th Streets, showing the Secretariat Building, the General Assembly Building and the Conference Building. The UN was built on land donated by John D. Rockefeller, Jr., and finished in 1952.

save the great Egyptian structures of antiquity and the European Gothic cathedrals of the Middle Ages can compare with the stupendous quality and quantity, or with the sheer beauty, of Manhattan's skyscrapers and bridges.

Because of these structures, New York is a city of views – ones which cannot be imitated by any other spot on earth. Besides the views from planes or helicopters, the best are from the **World Trade Center** and from the **Staten Island ferry**. The views from the **Empire State Building** and from **Rockefeller Center** are also stupendous, and that from the top of the **Statue of Liberty** and from **Ellis Island** are wonderful. There is a **Circle Line** boat every day which will show you the whole of Manhattan Island, the New Jersey bank

of the Hudson, the Bronx, Queens and Brooklyn from the water, as well as all the bridges. There's also another fine boat trip with magnificent views – the **Day Line** which steams up the Hudson to Bear Mountain State Park. You can also sail around the bay from **South Street Seaport**, or take one of the numerous sightseeing buses.

Learning and Culture. New York is also a great city of learning, with many front rank universities, colleges, research establishments and teaching hospitals. In the early 1960's when John Kennedy was President of the United States, New Yorkers used to joke that if you wanted to go to Washington you should go to Harvard and turn right: but if you wanted to go to Stockholm, seat of the Nobel Prize, you should go to Columbia and turn left...

*The **Met Life Building** and the **Grand Central Terminal** by night. In the 1960s everything possible was done to save Grand Central Station. Met Life, originally the **Pan Am Building**, was built on top of Grand Central almost as if it were symbolizing the supremacy of air over rail transport.*

Columbia is certainly the most prestigious of the city's institutions of learning, founded in 1754. But there are many others – New York University, Hunter College, City College, Fordham University, Brooklyn College and Yeshiwa University. The New York Public Library at 42nd Street and Fifth Avenue is perhaps the greatest municipal public library in the world, just as the Metropolitan Museum of Art is unquestionably the greatest municipal museum. The Morgan Library is one of the finest private libraries and the Julliard School of Music, the Brooklyn Academy of Music, and the Art Students League are equally renowned.

Museums. The list of the city's museums is almost endless: the Met's adjunct called **The Cloisters** at Fort Tyron Park on the northern end of Manhattan is a medieval treasure house. There

GRAND CENTRAL
TERMINAL

is the **Frick Museum**, also full of medieval and Renaissance art as well as more modern things. **The Museum of Modern Art**, the **Whitney**, the **Guggenheim**, together with the hundreds of galleries on the Upper East Side, in midtown, Soho and Tribeca give one an overview of modern art without equal anywhere in the world. Other museums are dotted all over the city – the **Brooklyn Museum**, the **Bronx Museum**, the **Jewish Museum**, the **New York Historical Society**, the **Museum of the City of New York**, the **Cooper-Hewitt**, the **Museum of Natural History**, the **Planetarium**, the **South Street Seaport**, the **Museum of the American Indian**, the **American Craft Museum**, the **Museum of Holography**, the **Museum of Broadcasting**, the **Sea, Air, Space Museum**, the **Asia Society**, the **Yivo Institute**, the **Museo Del Barrio**, and the **American Numismatic Society**.

The city which never sleeps. New York is a city of entertainment and of eating, maybe the best in the world in both categories, certainly the most varied. Besides Broadway with its magnificent neon lights, its forty-odd main theatres, and particularly its musical-comedies – almost a New York art form – there is Off-Broadway and Off-Off-Broadway, which means more than 150 smaller theatres offering shows most nights. Also available, as any visit to **Times Square** and its adjacent area will illustrate, are every variety of erotica, sex and drugs.

Ballet in New York is both classical and modern, many of the city's companies providing dance without parallel anywhere, such as the **Martha Graham Dance Company** at **City Center**, and the **Harlem Dance Theatre**. **The Metropolitan Opera**, **Carnegie Hall**, which offers pop, folk and

*The clock outside the **Grand Central Terminal Building**, crowned by the statues of **Mercury, Athena** and **Hercules**, and a view of the inside of the building.*

***Trump Tower** on 5th Avenue. The showpiece of a young real estate tycoon, the building has an atrium with an 80 foot waterfall.*

serious music, **Lincoln Center**, **Radio City Music Hall** and hundreds of movie houses playing the old and the new all provide something for everyone. Listening to live jazz is another New York nightime favorite, and there are many clubs all over the city which offer every variety. Still another wonderful New York institution is the piano-bar, many of which are in the major or minor hotels. These provide drinks, relaxing atmosphere and lovely music until late at night. Discos also exist all over the city, some of them Meccas for the aspiring Liza (and Liso...) Minnelli's of the world, while live dance music, particularly from the Caribbean and Latin America, can be unparalleled – often even in the country of origin.

*Some of New York's most famous skyscrapers. Even though the **Twin Towers** are higher than the **Empire State Building**, it is the latter which impresses the visitors most.*

Facing page, a panorama of the city seen from the Empire State Building.

*Panoramas of New York's stupendous cityscape, showing principally, in sequence, the **East River** and **United Nations Building**; the lower third of Manhattan Island with the **Hudson River, Upper New York Bay**, and twin towers of the **World Trade Center** in the distance; and the **Empire State Building**, with all the new business and residential skyscrapers of midtown Manhattan clustered around it, and to the north.*

Recreation in and around New York. For a major city, New York has remarkable and abundant nature nearby to which New Yorkers flock on weekends. The **Hudson Valley** itself is like a magnificent private park, its hundreds of miles of woods, hills and forests of easily accessible beauty. Northern New Jersey, southern New York State, Connecticut, to both the north and east of the city, all provide lovely unspoilt countryside and charming villages. New York has large city beaches at **Coney Island** and **Rockaway Park**. There is also available to the city almost the whole of the southern Long Island coast, some 90 miles long, including **Fire Island** and **Jones Beach**, the white sand and lack of pollution a wonderful change from the vastness of the metropolis. Sea fishing along the beaches of both the Atlantic and Long Island Sound is very popular.

On both sides of Long Island Sound, as well as in the New York bays and rivers themselves, there is also ample space for boating. Miles and miles of New Jersey beaches to the south are within a one – or two – hour drive of the city, their emptiness and cleanness unbelievable so near New York.

Inside the city the parks are all intensely used for jogging, roller-skating, cycling, picnicking, sun-bathing and public spectacles – particularly **Central Park** on Manhattan.

Wintertime provides indoor and outdoor skating, particularly in upstate New York, where there is also ample skiing and other winter sports.

Sports centers include the world-famous **Madison Square Garden**, site of many world-class boxing matches, as well as a number of race tracks and stadiums, particularly **Aqueduct**, **Yonkers**, **Belmont** and **Roosevelt Race Tracks** and **Yankee** and **Shea Stadiums**.

Scenes of Central Park, *Manhattan's principal park, with joggers and bicyclists exercising between the horse-drawn carriages of another era, and the looming cement and steel city towering over the trees.*

Food. There is probably no food in the world which can't be found in New York City, as well as a restaurant to serve it. The number of restaurants and the variety of foods is simply staggering. Manhattan alone has some fifteen thousand restaurants. Particularly rewarding in New York is seafood which, by European standards, is super-fresh, abundant and cheap. All the ethnic cuisines are also exciting, Chinese in particular, Indian, Vietnamese, Russian, Hungarian, Italian, and of course French. There are many excellent Japanese restaurants also, although they are almost never inexpensive. American cooking too can be surprisingly good, and recently **Cajun** cuisine from Louisiana has caught the city's fancy. New York City sandwiches are a meal in themselves. No visitor should leave the city without trying a pastrami sandwich, – available at good delicatessens, even late at night, a bagel with cream cheese and lox, a Nathan hot-dog, and, if you like alcohol, a cocktail in one of the more renowned bars or clubs.

Younger visitors. New York can also be wonderful for youngsters. Besides the enormous **Bronx Zoo** and the **Zoo** in Central Park, there's the **New York Aquarium**, **South Sea Seaport**, **Alice May Puppets**, **Aunt Len's Doll and Toy Museum**, the **Junior Museum of the Metropolitan Museum**, **13th St. Rep Theatre**, **the Magic Towne House**, **First All Children's Theatre**, as well as many other children's theatres, the **Brooklyn Children's Museum**, the **Staten Island Children's Museum**. Parades are a regular feature of New York life, and the young at heart always love them. Toy departments of the major shops, particularly **F.A.O. Schwartz**, are a wonderful experience for kids.

There are dance clubs which have children's or teenager's hours in the afternoon, and theatres which have children's concerts. Near the statue to Hans Christian Andersen in Central Park there are periodic readings of his fairy tales. Ice-skating in Rockefeller Center is elegant, but roller-skating, bicycle riding or jogging in Central

A typical New York residential block, with shops and restaurants on the street level.

Park are more universally enjoyed. And all the ferry and boatrides around the city are always very popular with youngsters.

History of New York. Giovanni da Verrazano, a Florentine, was the first modern European to see the future site of New York in 1524. But like the Vikings before him, who may have sailed into the bay, neither he nor his sponsors did anything about establishing a community. The Dutch did that in 1609 when Henry Hudson, an Englishman in Dutch employ, explored the bay and river which was given his name. From 1624 onwards, Europeans began to live on Governor's Island, and on Manhattan.

In 1626 the Dutch Governor, Peter Minuit, exchanged a heap of bright-colored junk, valued somewhere, sometime, by someone at the now legendary figure of $24 USA for Manhattan Island.

U.S. dollars, of course, didn't exist then, so the junk must have been sprinkled with a pinch of magic salt...

New Amsterdam, as it was called, remained Dutch until 1664 when the British fleet threatened the disliked mayor, Peter Stuyvesant, with extinction. Renamed **New York**, in 1686 it became the first town in the American colonies to be given a Royal Charter – that is a written agreement from the British government in London, giving the city the right to be self-governing in certain local matters, particularly trade.

During the War of Independence, and after, New York played a key role. It was not only the new country's first capital in 1789, but was host to the inauguration of the first President, George Washington. New York City was also the capital of the State of New York from 1784 to 1796.

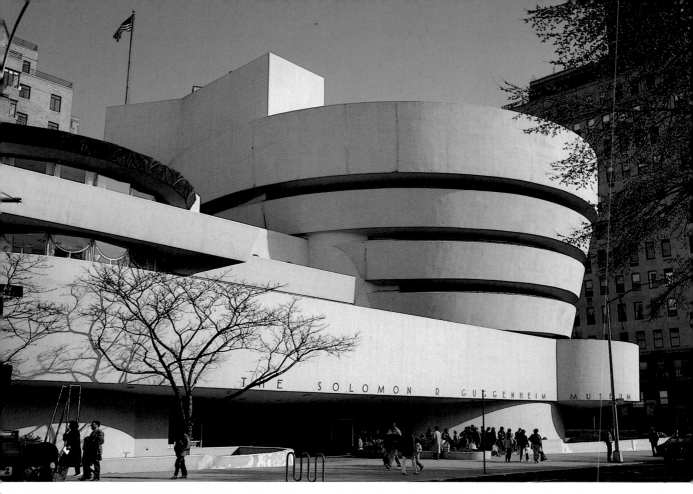

The Guggenheim Museum on 5th Avenue at 89th Street, built by Frank Lloyd Wright and opened in 1959 to house the pictures collected by the brothers, Solomon and Harry Guggenheim, New York financiers descended from a talented and generous Swiss family settled in New York City. Even among all the extraordinary architecture in Manhattan, this structure stands out as uniquely successful and organic.

Until 1898 New York meant Manhattan as it still does to people who live there. The island's citizens usually refer disdainfully to the other four boroughs, except of course when comparing them to New Jersey, which is considered even less gracefully...

Lincoln Center for the Performing Arts,
*on Columbus Avenue between 62nd and
65th Streets, the home of the Metropolitan
Opera, the New York Philharmonic, the
New York City Opera and Ballet, the
Julliard School, and numerous other
companies and institutions.*

New York has always been the
most populated US city. In 1790
the population was over 30,000.
By 1800 it was 60,000. During
the nineteenth century it grew
precipitously: by 1890 some
two-and-a-half million; by 1920
five-and-a-half million; by 1932
over seven million, more or less
the same official population it
still has today.

The Metropolitan Museum of Art on 5th Avenue between 80th and 84th Streets. The largest municipal museum in the world with some 248 separate galleries. It's practically impossible to see all the collections in a single visit.

Exhibits of pieces of the moon at the **Museum of Natural History**.

The crowded steps of the New York Public Library at 42nd Street and 5th Avenue, one of the many extraordinary book collections in the city, which include Butler and Low Libraries at **Columbia University**, and the **Morgan Library** at 29 E. 36th Street.

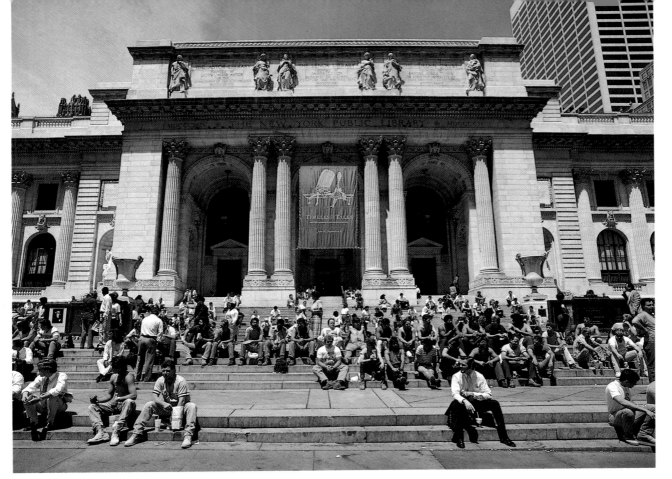

New York Today. The vastness of present New York in population, commerce and culture is hardly measureable. Brooklyn and Queens both have larger populations than Manhattan and would be major US cities in their own right were they not part of the City. The Bronx, too, has a population nearly the size of Manhattan. Staten Island has the lowest population of the five boroughs, but it has about two-and-a-half times the land-area of Manhattan.

Statistically, the official population figure for the five boroughs is between seven and eight million people and the area occupied about three hundred square miles. But both figures should be more than doubled when referring to the whole New York Metropolitan area. This includes not only the score of towns and millions of inhabitants along the New Jersey side of the Hudson, but the urban areas contiguous to the City, on Long Island, along the Connecticut coast line, in New York State north of the Bronx, and in the north of New Jersey. The total population of the metropolitan area is certainly between sixteen and eighteen million people.

Culturally, from the West Indians who coax miraculously happy rhythms out of empty steel cylinders in the streets, to Broadway and Lincoln Center, and from the crowded over-rich temples of the Metropolitan Museum and the Museum of Modern Art, to poor neglected artists all over the city, New York is without parallel anywhere on the globe.

How to see New York. The City has one of the best and most extensive public transportation systems in the world, using some sixty-five bridges and eighteen tunnels to join the five boroughs to each other and to the areas around the city.

The fastest way of getting around in the daytime traffic is unquestionably the subway. Each year some one billion people use the 373 kilometers of New York's subways – which hold the world record for the number of stations available to a city's public. This is an experience which many find unnecessary while some even find it distasteful. But if you want to know the true pulse of the city, you'll have to travel on the subway. Its amazing mixture of people, its crowds, its speed, its noise, its musicians and snack stands, its graffiti, combine to produce one of the places in New York City where no holds are barred culturally or socially. Buses are a slower way of travel, and from a ride in one of them along New York's main avenues, you can not only see the city

Some of New York's exciting night pop-art form called neon.

but often feel its friendliness. New York taxis are everywhere, efficient and fast, although the drivers, like taxi drivers all over the world – except perhaps in London – can be remarkably rude. If you have trouble, write down the driver's name and number and report him to the Taxi Commission. Taxi drivers are obligated to take you anywhere in the city but you may find that requests to go from Manhattan to certain parts of Brooklyn, Queens or the Bronx will meet with resistance, particularly if the driver doesn't speak much English – something which seems to

happen frequently in the city. As mentioned before, helicopters from East 34th Street on the river or from near the World Trade Center, give scenic rides over the city, the cost depending on the length of the flight. The **Circle Line**, the **Liberty Ferry**, the **Ellis Island Ferry**, and **Hudson River Day Line**, all have regular trips into New York Bay, to the Statue of Liberty and around Manhattan Island, as well as up the Hudson. And of course, the **Staten Island Ferry** will give you a view of the world's greatest and most exciting city you'll never forget.

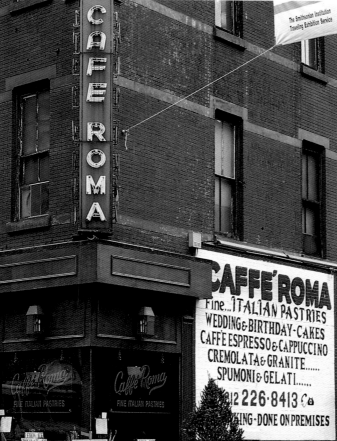

*All over New York are traces of great and small immigrations which have moved through the city. Some 3 to 5 million Italians arrived in New York between 1900 and 1930. Their businesses, houses and art can still be seen in many places in the city, particularly **Little Italy**, on the **Lower East Side**.*

***Chinatown** is another ethnic area, also on the Lower East Side, settled originally in part by laborers imported to help build the railroads who then refused to return to China. In the last 20 years it has grown enormously. Many people in Chinatown do not speak English, and in deference to this the New York telephone company has its telephone booths made in pagoda shapes with instructions in Chinese.*

New York is really its energetic people, moving about their magnificent city, working, creating, living, loving and dying. So the more you can wander the streets, visit the neighborhoods, the shops, eat in the restaurants and travel in and around the city, the more you savour its sights and its incredible buildings, the more you'll get to know New York.

It's one of the only cities in the US where you can walk and enjoy it. The finest long walk is down 5th Avenue from 96th Street, past the **Jewish Museum** at 92nd, past the **Guggenheim**, the **Metropolitan**, the **Frick**, **Emmanuel Synagogue**, the **Plaza Hotel**, past the chic shopping area in

the upper 50's, past **St Patrick's Cathedral** and **Rockefeller Center**, the **Museum of Modern Art**, the **New York Public Library**, on down to the **Empire State Building at 34th Street**. This walk will permit you to know New York well; it's about three miles long. Shorter walks along the principal cross streets of 96th, 86th, 72nd, 57th, 42nd, and 34th are also rewarding as is any stroll along any of the city's main arteries, particularly in the business districts, whether rich or poor.

There is no way a visitor can see all there is in New York, unless on several very filled-up days. Here, including sights already mentioned, are some of the many, many wonderful and interesting things to see in the world's most extraordinary city. And remember that New York belongs to everyone, to the visitor as much as to the immigrant or to the native-born New-Yorker, so enjoy yourself in the **Big Apple**. **New York City belongs to you too**!!

The arch in Washington Square at the bottom of 5th Avenue, center of Greenwich Village.

New York tenements. These small, very liveable town-houses, usually with two or four apartments per floor, and a single interior staircase, were all built during the great period of immigration from the 1880's until the 1920's. Hundreds of thousands have been pulled down particularly on the East Side along Second and Third Avenues, to make way for the new apartment towers. But large areas still remain, some now protected by conservation groups. Tenements always have exterior fire-escapes on the front or rear, in keeping with city ordinance, and are often called 'walk-ups' or 'brownstones'.

What to see in New York: Midtown. Most visitors who stay in hotels find themselves in the area known as Midtown, roughly from 34th Street to 59th Street, and both east and west of 5th Avenue. This area, together with that of the **Financial District**, is where most of the great skyscrapers are. Besides the **Empire State Building** on 5th Avenue at 34th Street, which has in it the **Guinness World Records Exhibit**, some of the buildings not to be missed are: the **Chrysler**

The **New York Stock Exchange**, the most important in the world, has its headquarters inside a building that looks like a Greek Corinthian temple, with **Integrity protecting the Works of Man** on the pediment.

Panorama overlooking **Manhattan**.

Following pages:

The World Trade Center. The twin towers are 411 meters high not counting the television antenna on the roof. The two exterior views are from **City Hall Park**, and from Brooklyn. The interior is in the covered observation deck on the 107th floor.

Building, 42nd Street and Lexington, the **Citicorp Center**, on E. 53rd Street, the **Pan American Building** with the **Grand Central Terminal** below it, on park between 42nd and 44th Street, **Lever House** on Park at 53rd, the **Segram Building**, opposite, the **Ford Foundation** on E. 43rd Street, the **A T & T Building** on 56th Street at Madison Avenue, the complex of **Rockefeller Center**, including the **RCA Building**, **Radio City Music Hall** and the central patio used for skating in the winter and a café in the summer, are all between 5th and 6th Avenues and between 49th and 51st Streets. Finally the **UN Headquarters**, the political organism for the various UN agencies (the Food and Agricultural Organisation in Rome, Unesco in Paris, the WHO and the ILO in Geneva, CEPAL in Santiago de Chile, and UNICEF) is on the East River between 42nd and 47th Streets on land donated by John D. Rockefeller, Jr.. Other landmarks in the Midtown area are **St Patrick's Cathedral** on 5th at 50th, the **Plaza Hotel**, again on 5th at 59th Street, **Japan House Gallery** on E.

47th Street, **Carnegie Hall** on W. 57th Street, the American sports palace on 33rd Street at 8th Avenue, **Madison Square Garden**, the **Museum of Modern Art** on 53rd Street, just west of 5th Avenue, and the magnificent neo-Classic building of the **New York Public Library** at 42nd Street and 5th Avenue. There is also the **Morgan Library** which is at number 29 E. 36th Street. Between about 42nd Street and 30th Street, going south along 7th Avenue is the area known as the Garment District, an extraordinary, teaming part of New York, in the daytime inhabited by hundreds of thousands of people who make and sell clothes. Many of the finest shops are in the Midtown area, particularly along 5th and Madison Avenues and in the streets between. The Midtown is also the night-time entertainment area, especially around **Times Square**, Broadway at 42nd Street.

Above 59th Street. **Central Park** occupies the whole center of Manhattan Island from 59th Street

Lower Manhattan seen from Brooklyn.

A municipal fireboat celebrating with jets of water under the Brooklyn Bridge.

The East River with the **Manhattan** and **Brooklyn Bridges** spanning it from Brooklyn to Manhattan.

New skyscrapers at the southern tip of Manhattan Island.

and 5th Avenue, to 110th Street, about two-and-a-half miles, and between 5th Avenue and Central Park West – which is a continuation of 8th Avenue. It's the great recreational lung of Manhattan and a lovely park to wander, picnic or exercise in. It contains a zoo, a famous merry-go-round for kids, a bridle path, a boating lake, a theatre and music mall, skating rinks, bowling areas, football fields, a reservoir and ponds to sail toy boats on. In the winter it's used for sledding, ice-skating and even for skiing. The streets north of 59th Street on both sides of the Park are primarily residential and so contain a great many cultural, educational and religious institutions. On the East Side are the **Museum of the City of New York** at 103rd Street on 5th

Manhattan skyscrapers *seen from Brooklyn, including the* **Empire State Building. The Staten Island Ferry Pier** *is at the left and the* **South Seaport Museum** *at the right.*

Views of the west side *of lower Manhattan from the Hudson River as it flows into the Upper Bay. Many of the buildings of the financial district are visible, the* **World Trade Center,** *the* **Empire State Building,** *and the* **South Seaport Museum.**

Avenue, the **Jewish Museum** on 5th and 92nd, the **Cooper-Hewitt** in Andrew Carnegie's mansion one block down on 91st Street at 5th, the **Guggenheim**, two blocks still further south at 89th Street, one of the most extraordinary buildings and collections of modern art in existence due to the generosity and culture of the two Guggenheim brothers, Solomon and Harry. Then there's the **Metropolitan Museum**, together with its adjunct, in Fort Tyron Park at the north end of Manhattan, called **The Cloisters**, the largest museum in the world. A bit farther south on Madison is the **Whitney Museum of American Art** at 75th Street and the wonderful **Frick Museum**, Henry Frick's house and collection, kept much as he left them, on 5th Avenue at 71st Street. Further south is the **Emmanuel Synagogue** at 5th Avenue and 65th. The residential area known as the Upper East Side is the chic-est

living quarter on Manhattan Island, especially along 5th and Park Avenues and in the streets in between them. Yuppy-land is along Lexington, 3rd, 2nd and 1st Avenues and the streets between. **Yorkville** is a famous ex-German immigrant area with traces of other ethnic groups nearby in Lennox Hill, particularly the Hungarians who lived along 2nd Avenue around 78th Street. A great part of northern Manhattan is occupied by **Harlem**, an area almost entirely lived in by black Americans who are the children, grandchildren and great-grandchildren of people who moved to New York to escape the racist treatment of black people in the southern part of the United States. Many areas contiguous to Harlem have been settled since World War II by immigrants from the Caribbean Island of Puerto Rico, particularly an area to the north of Yorkville, now called **Spanish Harlem** or **El Barrio**.

Preceding page:
Three views of the Brooklyn Bridge, *inaugurated in 1883. The bridge, which has separated roadway for cars to and from Manhattan and Brooklyn, also has a pedestrian walk on its top from which there are magnificent views of lower Manhattan.*

Lower Manhattan at night *across the East River from Brooklyn.*

The 110-story high **World Trade Center**; *a bird's-eye view of the* **Twin Towers**.

On the west side of Manhattan are **Columbia University** at 116th Street and Broadway, the vast neo-Gothic Protestant **Cathedral of St John the Divine**, still being built, at 110th Street and Columbus Avenue, **Audubon Terrace** which is at Broadway and 155th Street and includes an ornithological museum as well as the **Museum of the American Indian**. At 141st Street and Broadway there is **Aunt Len's Doll and Toy Museum**. The **Hayden Planetarium** is at Central Park West and 81st Street, the **American Museum of Natural History**, at 79th Street and Central Park West, the **New York Historical Society**, at 77th Street and Central Park West. Then there is the **Dakota Apartment Building** where many famous people have lived, including John Lennon, at 72nd and Central Park West, while the vast complex of the **Lincoln Center for the Performing Arts** and **Fordham University's Lincoln Campus** are between 65th and 60th Streets and between Columbus and Amsterdam Avenues.

North of Manhattan Island is the borough of the **Bronx** which has a wonderful **Zoo** and **Botanical** garden as well as the large **Van Cortlandt Park** with its Museum dedicated to the first native-born governor of New York City.

South of Midtown. There are the residential districts known as **Chelsea**, the **Lower East Side** and **Greenwich Village**. **Greenwich Village** is particularly attractive around **Sheridan** and **Washington Square**. The Lower East Side can be fascinating, boring, exciting or dangerous, depending on who and where you are and when you visit it. It's an area as famous for its Jewish Market in Orchard Street on Sundays, as it is for its drugs. Many Off-Off-Broadway theatres are also in the Greenwich Village area or on the Lower East Side.

Soho is south of Greenwich Village. The term stands for 'south of Houston Street' and the area is now the art gallery center of the world, there

The **East River** with the **bridges of Manhattan** and **Brooklyn**.

being literally hundreds of these. There is also, at number 11 Mercer Street, a **Museum of Holography.** To the east is **Little Italy**, once the center of the now very dispersed Italian community of New York. Below these areas is **Chinatown**, to the east, an area which was made almost a ghetto by city legislation. Worth visiting in Chinatown are not only some of the many restaurants but also the little **Chinese Museum**. To the west of Chinatown and south of Soho is the area called **Tribeca**, a term which is an abbreviation for 'triangle below Canal Street'. This is an area which is becoming fashionable among those who can't find space in Greenwich Village or in Soho. South of Tribeca and Chinatown is the Wall Street area known as the **Financial District**. Of all the skyscrapers which make up the southern tip of Manhattan's skyline, the earliest is the **Woolworth Building of 1911**, and the tallest is the **World Trade Center of 1974** with its incredible observation decks. There are

also in this area the **Staten Island**, **Ellis Island** and **Statue of Liberty Ferries**, the **South Street Seaport**, the **Downtown Heliport**, the **Downtown Whitney Museum**, the **New York Stock Exchange**, **Trinity Church**, dating from the early 19th century, **Battery Park**, the **Customs House**, and last but certainly not least, **City Hall**. Across the open East River which flows into New York's Upper Bay between the tip of Manhattan and Brooklyn is **Governor's Island**, a military base not open to the public, and beyond Governor's Island, **Brooklyn**.

Manhattan is joined to the areas around it by a number of significant bridges and tunnels. Seven of these cross over to Brooklyn or to Queens: the famous **Brooklyn Bridge**, completed after many difficulties in 1883, the **Manhattan**, **Williamsburg**, **Queensborough**, and **Triborough Bridges**; as well as the **Brooklyn Battery Tunnel** and the **Queens Midtown Tunnel**. There is also a cable car from 59th Street and 2nd Avenue to **Roosevelt Island** in the East River, a recently developed residential area. The other two main New York bridges are the **Verrazano Bridge** from Brooklyn to Staten Island, the second longest suspension bridge in the world and the **George Washington Bridge** from Upper Manhattan to New Jersey, the fourth longest after the Golden Gate in San Francisco. Between Manhattan and New Jersey are two tunnel systems – the Holland Tunnel and the Lincoln Tunnel.

The Borough of Brooklyn, by itself is as large as a major United States city, and the view from Brooklyn Heights over towards Manhattan is wonderful. In Brooklyn, the **Brooklyn Museum** and the **Brooklyn Botanical Gardens**, as well as the **Aquarium** are all worth visiting. North of Brooklyn is **Queens** where New York's largest airports, **La Guardia** and **JFK** are located. It's also the site of some lovely New York beaches and of a large wildlife area at **Jamaica Bay**.

To the west, almost part of New Jersey, across Upper New York Bay, is **Staten Island**, the least populated of the five boroughs, although two-and-a-half times the size of Manhattan. Much to its inhabitants' joy, the island is still greatly under-developed. The village museum of **Richmondtown Restoration** is interesting to visit as there is the **Staten Island Zoo** with its exceptional collection of reptiles. There is also a **Tibetan Museum**. There are also two other islands in New York's Upper Bay, both small but both very important. **Ellis Island** was the landing place for some 25 million future Americans who where 'processed' before being allowed to cross the Bay to New York. Restoration of the buildings on the island is now almost complete. A **Museum of Immigration** is being installed. **Liberty Island** also has a museum and its famous statue is the ultimate tribute to the new life, the new city and the new country which all those immigrants made.

A sweeping panorama of New York.

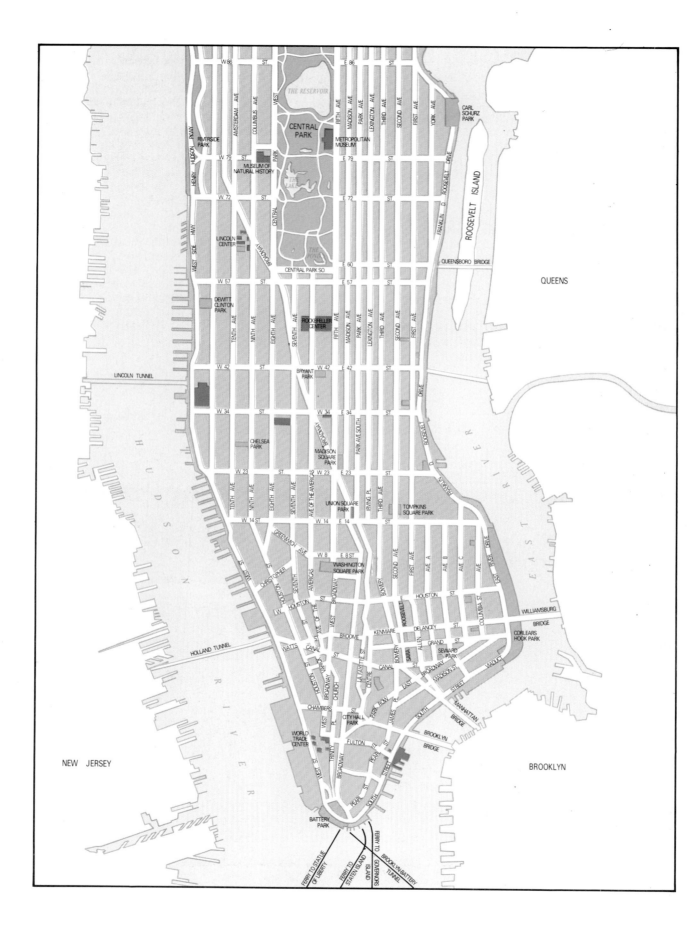